Cool
Pacific Coast
Cooking

Easy and Fun Regional Recipes

Alex Kuskowski

visit us at www.abdopublishing.com

Published by ABDO Publishing Company, a division of ABDO,
P.O. Box 398166, Minneapolis, Minnesota 55439. Copyright ©
2014 by Abdo Consulting Group, Inc. International copyrights
reserved in all countries. No part of this book may be
reproduced in any form without written permission from
the publisher. Super SandCastle™ is a trademark and logo of
ABDO Publishing Company.

Printed in the United States of America, North Mankato,
Minnesota
062013
092013

Editor: Liz Salzmann
Content Developer: Nancy Tuminelly
Cover and Interior Design and Production:
Colleen Dolphin, Mighty Media, Inc.
Food Production: Desirée Bussiere
Photo Credits: Colleen Dolphin, Shutterstock

The following manufacturers/names appearing in this book
are trademarks: Argo®, Heinz®, Holland House®, Marukan®,
McCormick®, Old London®, Oregon®, Roundy's®, Thai Kitchen®

Library of Congress Cataloging-in-Publication Data

Kuskowski, Alex.
  Cool Pacific Coast cooking : easy and fun regional recipes /
Alex Kuskowski.
      pages cm -- (Cool USA cooking)
  Audience: Ages 8-12.
  Includes index.
  ISBN 978-1-61783-831-6
  1. Cooking, American--California style--Juvenile literature.
  2. Cooking, American--Pacific Northwest style--Juvenile
literature. I. Title.
  TX715.2.C34K87 2014
  641.59794--dc23
                                        2013001907

Safety First!

Some recipes call for activities or
ingredients that require caution. If you
see these symbols ask an adult for help!

HOT STUFF!
This recipe requires the use
of a stove or oven. Always use
pot holders when handling hot
objects.

SUPER SHARP!
This recipe includes the use of
a sharp **utensil** such as a knife
or grater.

NUT ALERT!
Some people can get very sick if
they eat nuts. If you are cooking
with nuts, let people know!

Cuisine Cooking

Each regional recipe can have a lot of
versions. Many are **unique** to the cook.
The recipes in this book are meant to
give you just a taste of regional cooking.
If you want to learn more about one
kind of cooking, go to your local library
or search online. There are many great
recipes to try!

Contents

Discover Pacific Coast Eats!

Pacific Coast **cuisine** is a fusion of flavors! The recipes combine ingredients from different cuisines including Chinese, Hawaiian, and Mexican. Mixing these styles can create **unique** dishes that taste great.

On the Pacific Coast many fresh ingredients are **available**. Seafood, vegetables, and fruits are all harvested nearby. Fresh foods make it easy for people to experiment with fun flavors.

There is a lot to learn about foods from the Pacific Coast. Use the recipes in this book to have your own feast. Try them all, or make up your own. Grab a chef's hat, it's time for a cooking adventure!

Learn About the Pacific Coast

Regional cooking has a lot to do with where the ingredients and recipes are from. Every region has its own **culture**. What do you know about Pacific Coast culture and food?

Washington

More cherries, apples, and raspberries grow here than in any other state.

Alaska

Alaska has a lot of fish. Most of America's salmon, crab, halibut, and herring come from Alaska.

Oregon

In Oregon, people love fruits. Pears, plums, apples, prunes, and cherries have been grown here for more than a hundred years!

Hawaii

The native culture in Hawaii is **Polynesian**. One well-known tradition is the luau. They serve roasted pig, salmon tomato salad, and coconut cake. It's a party!

California

This state grows more than half of all fruits and nuts in the entire country! More strawberries and almonds are from California than any other state.

The Basics

Ask Permission

Before you cook, ask **permission** to use the kitchen, cooking tools, and ingredients. If you'd like to do something yourself, say so. Just remember to be safe. If you would like help, ask for it. Always ask for help using a stove or oven.

Be Prepared

- Be organized. Knowing where everything is makes cooking easier and safer.

- Read the directions all the way through before you start. Remember to follow the directions in order.

- The most important ingredient in great cooking is preparation! Set out all your ingredients before starting.

Be Neat and Clean

- Start with clean hands, clean tools, and a clean work surface.

- Tie back long hair so it stays out of the food.

- Wear comfortable clothing. Roll up long sleeves.

Be Smart, Be Safe

- Never work in the kitchen if you are home alone.

- Always have an adult close by for hot jobs, such as using the oven or the stove.

- Have an adult around when using a sharp tool, such as a knife or grater. Always be careful when using them!

- Remember to turn pot handles toward the back of the stove. That way you won't accidentally knock them over.

Cool Cooking Terms

Peel

Peel means to remove the skin, often with a peeler.

Chop

Chop means to cut into small pieces.

Boil

Boil means to heat liquid until it begins to bubble.

Dice/Cube

Dice and *cube* mean to cut something into small squares.

Slice

Slice means to cut food into pieces of the same thickness.

Grate

Grate means to shred something into small pieces using a grater.

Whisk

Whisk means to beat quickly by hand with a whisk or a fork.

Drain

Drain means to remove liquid using a strainer or colander.

The Tool Box

Here are some of the tools that you'll need for the recipes in this book.

8 × 8-inch baking dish

colander

cutting board

frying pan

measuring cups & spoons

mixing bowls

pot holders

pie pan

saucepan

spatula

toaster

whisk

The Ingredients

Here are some of the ingredients that you'll need for the recipes in this book.

alfalfa sprouts	almond extract	apple cider vinegar
avocado	balsamic vinegar	bread crumbs
cilantro	coconut milk	cornstarch
crushed red pepper flakes	cumin	Dijon mustard

garlic

olive oil

Parmesan cheese

parsley

pistachio nuts

red onion

red pepper

rice vinegar

salmon

scallions

soba noodles

soy sauce

sweet cherries

vanilla extract

zucchini

13

Veggie Brunch Special

Wake up with this breakfast dish!

Makes 4 servings

Ingredients

¼ cup vegetable oil
2 cups chopped onion
1 teaspoon minced garlic
1 cup chopped red pepper
1½ cups diced tomato
1 cup sliced zucchini
1 teaspoon salt
1 teaspoon black pepper
1 teaspoon cumin
15-ounce can lima beans, drained
¼ cup parsley, chopped
4 eggs
1 cup grated cheddar cheese

Tools

sharp knife
cutting board
measuring cups
measuring spoons
grater
frying pan
spatula
8 × 8-inch baking dish
mixing bowl
whisk
pot holders

*hot!
*sharp!

1   Preheat the oven to 400 degrees.

2   Put the oil and onion in a frying pan. Stir while cooking over medium heat for 5 minutes. Add the garlic, red pepper, tomatoes, zucchini, salt, black pepper, and cumin.

3   Turn the heat to low and cook for 15 more minutes. Stir occasionally. Add the beans and cook for 10 minutes. Stir frequently. Stir in the parsley. Remove the pan from the heat.

4   Put the veggie mixture in a baking dish.

5   Whisk the eggs together in a mixing bowl. Pour them over the veggie mixture. Sprinkle the cheddar cheese on top.

6   Bake 20 minutes. Enjoy with a glass of milk or juice for a yummy take on breakfast!

California Guacamole

Try this fast and simple chip dip!

Makes 4 servings

Ingredients

2 avocados

¼ cup cottage cheese

½ cup chopped tomato

½ cup chopped cilantro

2 tablespoons chopped toasted pistachio nuts

¼ teaspoon crushed red pepper flakes

1 clove minced garlic

1 tablespoon lime juice

½ teaspoon salt

Tools

sharp knife

cutting board

spoon

measuring cups

measuring spoons

medium mixing bowl

fork

mixing spoon

*sharp!
*nuts!

1 Cut the avocados in half. Remove the pits. Scoop the avocados out of their skins. Put them in a mixing bowl.

2 Mash the avocados with a fork.

3 Add the remaining ingredients. Stir until everything is just mixed.

4 Serve immediately with fresh veggies, pitas, or tortilla chips for dipping.

Avocado Orange Sandwich

A tasty, toasted light lunch!

Makes 2 servings

Ingredients

1 avocado
4 slices sourdough bread
2 tablespoons mayonnaise
1 orange, peeled
½ cup alfalfa sprouts
1 teaspoon balsamic vinegar
1 red onion, sliced
8 slices Swiss cheese

Tools

measuring cups
measuring spoons
sharp knife
cutting board
spoon
toaster

*sharp!

1. Cut the avocado in half. Remove the pit and skin. Cut the avocado into thin slices.

2. Lightly toast all four pieces of bread. Spread mayonnaise on one side of each piece.

3. Put Swiss cheese on two of the pieces of toast. Put orange sections on the Swiss cheese.

4. Add layers of avocado slices, sprouts, and onion on top of the oranges.

5. **Drizzle** balsamic vinegar over each **sandwich**.

6. Put one of the remaining pieces of toast on top of each sandwich. Enjoy a healthy, flavorful lunch!

Tip: To remove the avocado skin, gently scoop under the avocado with a spoon.

Chinese Noodles & Peanut Sauce

Add the perfect kick to your pasta!

Makes 2 servings

Ingredients

8 oz package soba noodles
½ cup natural peanut butter
½ cup coconut milk
2 tablespoons soy sauce
2 tablespoons brown sugar
3 cloves minced garlic
1 teaspoon apple cider vinegar
1 tablespoon chopped cilantro
¼ teaspoon hot pepper sauce
 (optional)
¼ cup diced red pepper
¼ cup chopped scallions

Tools

measuring cups
saucepan
colander
mixing bowls
mixing spoon
measuring spoons
whisk
sharp knife
cutting board

*hot!
*sharp!
*nuts!

1 Boil 3 cups of water in a saucepan. Cook the noodles according to the instructions on the package. Drain the noodles and put them in a medium mixing bowl.

2 Put the peanut butter, coconut milk, and ¼ cup hot water in a separate mixing bowl. Stir until combined.

3 Add the soy sauce, brown sugar, vinegar, cilantro, and hot pepper sauce. Whisk mixture together.

4 Pour the peanut sauce over the noodles. Stir to coat the noodles. Sprinkle on the red pepper and scallions. Divide noodles onto two serving plates. Dig in!

Even Cooler

This peanut sauce is great with anything! Try dipping vegetables or **grilled shrimp** in it.

Golden State Potato Salad

Grab a bowl before it's gone!

Makes 4 servings

Ingredients

5 red potatoes
1 tablespoon salt
½ cup grated Parmesan cheese
3 cloves garlic, minced
¼ cup chopped parsley
¼ cup olive oil
1 tablespoon Dijon mustard
2 tablespoons rice vinegar
3 tablespoons mayonnaise
1 teaspoon black pepper
3 scallions, chopped

Tools

large saucepan
mixing spoon
measuring cups
measuring spoons
sharp knife
cutting board
colander
mixing bowls

*hot!
*sharp!

1   Cut the potatoes into small pieces.

2   Put the potatoes, salt, and 4 cups of water in a saucepan. Bring to a boil. Reduce the heat to medium-low. Cover and cook until you can easily pierce the potatoes with a knife. It takes about 15 minutes.

3   Drain the potatoes. Let them cool completely.

4   Put the cheese, garlic, parsley, olive oil, mustard, vinegar, mayonnaise, and black pepper in a mixing bowl. Stir.

5   Add the potatoes and scallions to the cheese mixture. Toss to coat. Chow down on this California classic!

Perfect Salmon Burgers

Try a burger with a fun new twist!

Makes 5 servings

Ingredients

14.75-ounce can salmon
2 tablespoons olive oil
1 medium onion, chopped
1 clove garlic, minced
⅔ cup bread crumbs
2 eggs
¼ cup chopped parsley
2 tablespoons lemon juice
1½ tablespoons Dijon mustard
non-stick cooking spray
5 hamburger buns

Tools

measuring cups
measuring spoons
fork
frying pan
medium mixing bowl
mixing spoon
spatula
sharp knife
cutting board

*hot!
*sharp!

1 Drain the salmon. Use a fork to break it up. This is called flaking.

2 Put the onion and 1 tablespoon olive oil in a frying pan over medium-high heat. Cook until the onion turns clear. It takes about 5 minutes. Remove the pan from the heat and let it cool.

3 Put the onion in a mixing bowl. Add the garlic, bread crumbs, eggs, parsley, lemon juice, mustard, salmon, and 1 tablespoon olive oil. Mix with your hands.

4 Form the mixture into 5 **patties**. Refrigerate them for 1 hour.

5 Coat the frying pan with cooking spray. Heat the pan over medium-high heat. Cook the patties for 5 minutes. Flip them over. Cook them for 5 more minutes.

6 Put each patty on a bun. Serve with lemon wedges.

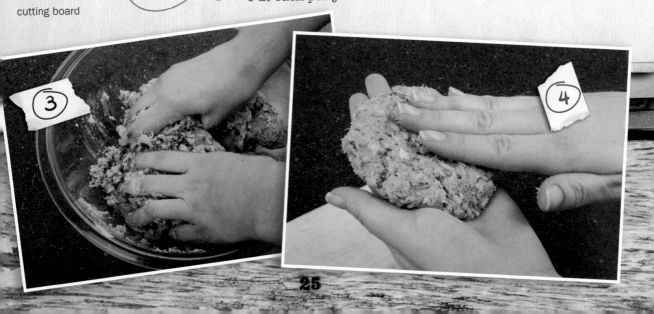

Hawaiian Luau Dessert

A cool, sweet party dessert!

Makes 24 servings

Ingredients

1 can coconut milk
¼ cup sugar
5 tablespoons cornstarch
½ teaspoon vanilla extract
3 kiwis, peeled and sliced

Tools

measuring cups
measuring spoons
saucepan
mixing spoon
8 × 8-inch baking dish
sharp knife
cutting board

*hot!
*sharp!

1 Put ¼ cup coconut milk in a saucepan. Stir in the sugar and cornstarch.

2 Heat on the stove over medium-low heat for 1 minute.

3 Add the rest of the coconut milk and ¾ cup water. Cook for 10 minutes while stirring constantly. Add the vanilla.

4 Remove the pan from the heat. Stir for 10 more minutes.

5 Pour the mixture into the baking dish. Chill in the refrigerator for 1 hour. Cut into pieces and serve with kiwi slices.

Even Cooler!

Try serving this dessert with other fruits, such as berries or sliced pineapple!

Pacific Coast Cherry Pie

This juicy pie will melt in your mouth!

Makes 8 servings

Ingredients

2 9-inch refrigerated
  pie crusts
2 cups pitted, dark,
  sweet cherries
¼ cup cherry juice
⅓ cup sugar
⅓ cup brown sugar
¼ cup flour
¼ teaspoon almond extract
1 tablespoon butter,
  cut into pieces

Tools

pie pan
pot holders
measuring cups
measuring spoons
large mixing bowl
mixing spoon
knife

*hot!
*sharp!
*nuts!

1 Preheat the oven to 425 degrees.

2 Put one pie crust in the bottom of the pie pan.

3 Put the cherries, juice, sugar, brown sugar, flour, and almond extract in a bowl. Stir well. Let the mixture sit for 15 minutes.

4 Pour the cherry filling mixture into the pie pan. Arrange the pieces of butter on top.

5 Place the second pie crust over the top. Cut a few slits in the top pie crust.

6 Bake for 25 to 30 minutes, or until the filling begins to bubble. Let the pie cool. Then cut it into slices and serve!

Conclusion

Now you know how to make some wonderful Pacific Coast dishes! Did you learn anything about Pacific Coast **cuisine**? Did you try any new foods? Everywhere you go there are new foods to experience.

From coast to coast, the United States is a land of **delicious** dishes! East Coast, Pacific Coast, Gulf Coast, Midwest, South, and West are the main regions of US cuisine. Try them all to get a taste of the United States. See if one is your favorite!

Glossary

available – able to be had or used.

cuisine – a style of preparing and presenting food.

culture – the behavior, beliefs, art, and other products of a particular group of people.

delicious – very pleasing to taste or smell.

drizzle – to pour in a thin stream.

grill – to cook food on a grill.

patty – a round, flat cake made with chopped food.

permission – when a person in charge says it's okay to do something.

Polynesian – from any of the islands in the central and south Pacific Ocean, including Hawaii.

sandwich – two pieces of bread with a filling, such as meat, cheese, or peanut butter, between them.

shrimp – a small shellfish often caught for food.

unique – different, unusual, or special.

utensil – a tool used to prepare or eat food.

version – a different form or type from the original.

Web Sites

To learn more about regional US cooking, visit ABDO Publishing Company online at www.abdopublishing.com. Web sites about easy and fun regional recipes are featured on our Book Links page. These links are routinely monitored and updated to provide the most current information available.

Index